ANIMAL STORY

BIG CAT
SUMMER

by Dougal Dixon

With thanks to our consultant, Tricia Holford, The Born Free Foundation

WATERBIRD BOOKS

Columbus, Ohio

ANIMAL STORY

BIG CAT
SUMMER

 **Children's Publishing**

This edition published in the United States of America in 2004 by
Waterbird Books
an imprint of McGraw-Hill Children's Publishing,
a Division of The McGraw-Hill Companies
8787 Orion Place
Columbus, Ohio 43240-4027

www.MHkids.com

Library of Congress Cataloging-in-Publication Data is on file with the publisher.

First published in Great Britain in 2004 by *ticktock* Media Ltd.,
Unit 2 Orchard Business Centre, North Farm Road, Tunbridge Wells, Kent TN3 3XF.
Text and illustrations © 2004 *ticktock* Entertainment Ltd.
we would like to thank: Downs Matthews, Director Emeritus, Polar Bears International, Jean Coppendale and Elizabeth Wiggans.
Every effort has been made to trace the copyright holders, and we apologize in advance for any unintentional omissions.
We would be pleased to insert the appropriate acknowledgements in any subsequent edition of this publication.

Printed in China

1-57768-879-1

1 2 3 4 5 6 7 8 9 10 TTM 09 08 07 06 05 04

The McGraw·Hill Companies

CONTENTS

LEAH, THE AFRICAN LIONESS

Leah lies in the dappled sunlight. She stretches out her tan-colored body. Nearby, her three cubs are playing. Leah is an African lioness, and she is safe and secure with the rest of the lions with whom she lives. This group is called a **pride**.

Close by stands the majestic Pantha, the pride's dominant male. He gazes out over the savanna, looking for food and for danger. Pantha is the father of Leah's cubs. He keeps all of the lions safe.

The pride is quite small. It is just Leah, her four sisters, Pantha, and his second-in-command, a younger male, and six cubs. Leah's three cubs are eight weeks old. They still drink her milk. Sometimes her sister's three cubs also drink her milk.

The cubs playfully stalk and pounce on the black tuft at the end of Leah's twitching tail. For now, they do not need to worry about finding their own food. When they are adults though, they will have to hunt for themselves. Chasing tails is good hunting practice for the future.

Leah and her pride live on the grasslands of Africa. In the wet season, torrential rain sweeps across the savanna. In the dry season, the landscape can be as dry as a desert.

Yellow grasses stretch away to the horizon, with bushes and thorn trees dotted here and there.

The grasslands are home to many herds of hoofed animals. The wildebeests, antelope, and zebras that live here have adapted to this environment. They can digest the tough grass. They graze on the plains, traveling, or *migrating,* from place to place to find food. Small groups of giraffes nibble on the thorn trees.

Leah and her pride hunt the herds of grassland animals, but, the lions are not the only hunters in this area. Sometimes cheetahs

appear and chase speeding antelope. Packs of yapping spotted hyenas are often found here too. They wait to make a kill or for the chance to scavenge some food.

LIFE IN THE PRIDE

Darkness has fallen and the air is cooler. It is time to hunt.

The six cubs are left with one of the females. Two of the lionesses stalk out into the darkness, silently circling a group of zebra. Leah and her other sister move into position, ready to move in on, or *ambush,* their prey. A breeze carries the scent of the two female lions toward the herd. As soon as the zebras detect the smell, they instinctively know that it means danger. The zebras stampede away from the two female lions. This is exactly what the pride had anticipated the zebras would do. Snorting and panicking, the herd of zebras runs straight into Leah and her other sister.

Leah suddenly leaps, dragging
a passing zebra into the dusty soil.
She seizes it by the neck, her strong
jaw and huge teeth crushing her victim.
The hunt is a success.

The two male lions move in to begin the
feast, while the lionesses and cubs wait
for their turn to eat.

When the family is not hunting or relaxing, Pantha patrols the boundaries of their home range.

Their home range is the area where the pride lives over the course of many months or years. Pantha leaves his scent on the trees and rocks and makes claw marks in the trunks of the trees. He does this to let other lions know that the territory belongs to his pride. At sunset, Pantha's huge territorial roar can be heard across the plains, telling other lions in the area to stay away.

Pantha is larger and heavier than the females, and his thick mane makes him look even bigger. He has been leading the pride for four years, but Pantha is getting old. His eyesight is failing, and he cannot move as quickly as he used to.

One evening, when he is away from the rest of the pride, he is suddenly surrounded by a pack of spotted hyenas.

The hyenas close in on Pantha, coming at him from all sides. The group of hyenas bite and nip at Pantha.

There is nothing he can do to fight back. Pantha is doomed.

Back at the pride, Leah and her sisters sniff the night air. Where is their leader?

A NEW LEADER

It is as if the news has spread out across the plains.
Leah's pride is without a leader. By the next day,
there is a stranger prowling around their territory.

A new male has appeared. He is a large, fierce lion covered
in scars from fighting. The young male in Leah's pride
does not stand a chance of surviving in the pride.
He is driven away by the new lion.

Now, the pride's cubs are in great danger.
When a new male takes over a pride,
he wants the pride to be his.
He will not care for
another male's cubs.

Within hours, the lion has killed Leah's sister's cubs. Within a few days, though, she will have completely forgotten her cubs. She will be ready to mate with the new dominant male.

Leah is not so easily dominated, though. She fights face to face with the new male. She snarls and paws the air as soon as he comes close to her babies. After a while, the huge male gives in. Leah's cubs will survive the takeover.

It is the end of the dry season, and prey is hard to find. Soon, the rains will come, and fresh, new grass will grow. Then, the herds of wildebeests, antelope, and zebras will return to Leah's territory.

But this year when the rains come, the herds do not follow. The new dominant male is good at searching out prey, but something is keeping the herds away.

When there is plenty of food, lions need to hunt only every few days. Now, Leah leads the other lionesses out day after day, with little success. Hunger is beginning to set in.

One morning, several strange lionesses approach Leah's pride. They are hungry, too. The strangers circle closer and closer, but Leah stands her ground. When she fought with the new male, she established her dominance in the pride. Now, she attacks the strangers, and the rest of the pride follows her lead.

Even though it is the rainy season, the herds of wildebeests and antelope still have not come. There is no food for the pride.

Day after day, the hungry pride peers out from the dripping grass, over the empty savannah.

TROUBLE ON THE SAVANNAH

Time is running out. Leah and her family will have to travel farther to search for food.

As the lions roam across the deserted, wet grassland, they come across something they have never seen before.

They come across a huge canyon full of machines and loud rumbling noises. A mining company is looking for valuable minerals and metals in the ground. Hundreds of people are working in the canyon. Hunters and trappers are on the plain hoping to catch animals to feed the people. The loud noise and workers' activities have scared away the migrating herds of wildebeests and antelope.

The workers have brought their own food, too. There is a herd of cattle in a large pen. The pride watches from a distance. Leah has never seen cattle before. To an underfed lioness with starving cubs, the cattle look like prey.

The pride waits. As the sun begins to set, the people stop their work and go into the temporary buildings and tents around their camp.

Leaving the cubs to be cared for by one of the females, the pride creeps into the camp. They sniff around. They want to get to the cattle in the pen.

The fence is strong enough to keep the cattle in, but it is not high enough to keep the starving lions out.

One by one, the lions leap the fence and land inside the cattle pen. But it is a clumsy attack. The startled cattle begin making loud noises. Leah and the others leap and lunge, and several of the smaller cattle are killed.

The lions do not have time to eat. The noise has alerted the people. Lights come on around the camp. Suddenly, the air is full of shouting and the sounds of guns firing. Still hungry, Leah and the pride escape.

THE PRIDE MUST ESCAPE

The miners are angry at the loss of their cattle. Leah and her pride are hungrier than ever, and now they are in serious danger.

The miners set out with flaming torches, tracker dogs, and guns. They want to make sure that lions do not attack their cattle again.

Leah watches from the distance. She has excellent night vision. She would be able to see the people approaching even if they were not carrying torches. Now, the dogs have picked up the lions' scent. They are howling and pulling at their leashes. Leah turns and leads her cubs and the other lionesses away.

The male lion does not retreat, though. He stands his ground. As the human beings approach, the male lion charges at them. The male lion expects the group of people to panic and flee just as the antelope and zebras did. They do not. The people have guns. The male lion does not return to the pride.

In many parts of Africa, lions and people now compete for space, as farming and industry take over the lions' natural habitat.

Without the grassland, the herds of zebras, wildebeests and antelope disappear. Desperate lions are sometimes forced to attack the cattle on farms.

Now that human beings have taken over Leah's old territory, it is too dangerous for Leah and the pride to stay there. They will have to move on to search for food.

On the first day of a long trip, the lionesses manage to catch a warthog. It does not provide enough food for five lionesses and three cubs.

After several days, they come across an area with a few small herds of antelope. The area looks like a good place to stop, but there is already a pride of lions living there. The other lions are determined to hold on to their territory. Leah and her family are forced to move on.

At a waterhole, the lionesses and cubs stop for a drink. But, elephants are bathing there with their calves. Lions are not a danger to adult elephants. But elephants do not want to risk the safety of their young. To protect their young, the elephants charge. Leah and her family are forced to run away again.

A NEW LIFE

Slowly, the landscape around the pride changes. The grasses become shorter as the land rises into rolling hills. Farther on, the hills become mountains.

It is very unusual for a family of lions to travel like this, but their old territory can no longer support them. Leah must find a new place for the pride to live.

Then, early one morning, as the mist clears, the pride wanders onto on a vast plain. Yellow grasses wave in the morning breeze. In the distance, they see herds of antelope and zebras. Nearby, giraffes nibble from scattered thorn trees.

The pride will be safe here. They have crossed over into a special place called a *wildlife reserve*. The land here is set aside for the animals. It will not be disturbed by miners, hunters, or anyone else.

Leah lies in the dappled sunlight. She stretches out her tan-colored body. Nearby, her three new cubs are playing.

Leah's babies, who made the long trek with her that summer, have grown up. Her daughter stays close, but her two sons have left the pride. They now live with several other young males in a small bachelor group. One day, they will lead prides of their own.

In the last 18 months, Leah's group has settled into life on the wildlife reserve. Eventually, two new males joined the pride. When her original cubs no longer needed her, Leah mated with the dominant male.

Now, the family sleeps for up to 20 hours each day and hunts together at night. They prey on herds of hoofed animals that live on the reserve. Tourists come to photograph the animals. The farmers who live here understand that they need to share the reserve with the lions.

Leah and the pride are safe and secure in their new territory.

LION FACT FILE

*The lion's scientific name is **Panthera leo** ("Panthera" is "lion" in Greek, and "leo" is "lion" in Latin).* Lions are members of the felidae, or cat family. Two subspecies of African lion, the Barbary lion and the Cape lion are now extinct, and the Asiatic lion (from Asia) is critically endangered.

THE WORLD OF THE AFRICAN LION

African lions are found in the areas marked on the map. Lion populations living in protected wildlife reserves are doing well. Elsewhere in Africa, lions exist only in small numbers, and these populations are in danger of disappearing.

HABITAT

- Lions live on the African savannah, where it is warm all year round. Their main habitat is among the scatterings of trees and bushes.

- Lions share their world with other large carnivores such as cheetahs, leopards, and hyenas.

- The African grasslands support vast herds of prey animals such as zebras, wildebeests, antelope, and buffalo. They migrate from place to place to find the most lush areas of grass.

- In the dry season (the winter), the plant life dies off. In the rainy season (the summer), the plant-life bursts back into life.

- Unlike most plants that grow from the tip, grass stems grow from the base. This means that when the grass is eaten by animals or damaged by dry weather conditions or fire, it can regrow.

Lions are found in the west of Africa in Cameroon, Nigeria and Senegal.

Healthy lion populations can be found in protected areas in South Africa, Botswana, Namibia, Zambia, Zimbabwe, Mozambique, Tanzania, Kenya, Uganda, Ethiopia, and the east of Sudan.

PHYSICAL CHARACTERISTICS

FEMALE

Height: 3.5 feet

Length: 8.25 feet
(including tail)

Maximum weight:
400 pounds

MALE

Height: 4 feet

Length: 6.5–9.75 feet
(including tail)

Maximum weight:
530 pounds

- Scientists believe a male lion's mane helps him to look larger and more impressive to other males. It may also help to protect his throat during fights.

- A male's mane begins to grow when he is about two years old.

- All lions have black tufts of hair at the end of their tails.

- Lions have little dots on their muzzles around their whiskers. The dots stay the same throughout the lion's life and are as individual as human beings' fingerprints.

- Cubs are born with slightly spotted coats. The spots begin to fade when the cubs are about three months old.

- In the wild, lions can live for about 15 to 18 years. But, most of them live for only about 5 to 10 years.

AFRICAN GRASSLANDS FOOD WEB

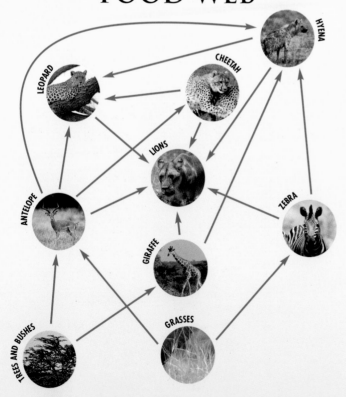

This food web shows how the animals and plants living on the African grasslands depend on each other for food. The arrows in the web mean "give food to."

DIET

- Lions commonly eat wildebeests, zebras, antelope, and warthogs. They will also catch small animals such as rabbits.

- Lions hunt in groups by stalking, surrounding, and ambushing their prey. Sometimes, a group of lions working together, will catch a big animal, such as a buffalo.

- Lions get their food both by hunting and by stealing, or *scavenging*, meat from other carnivores.

- Only about 30% of lion hunts are successful!

- A lion can eat as much as 60 pounds of meat at one time. A normal meal is about 15 pounds.

- After a hunt, the males get to eat first, then the lionesses, and finally the cubs.

- Lions will eat their whole kill in one sitting, but then may not eat again for a few days.

- Lions lap up water with their tongues, but only a little at a time. It can take a lion up to ten minutes to quench its thirst.

BEHAVIOR AND SENSES

- Lions are the only cats that live in large multi-female groups.

- Prides can have as few as three members or as many as 50. Most prides have about 15 members.

- Usually the lionesses in a pride are related. They are sisters, daughters, mothers, and grandmothers.

- Males leave the pride when they are two to four years old. Brothers will normally stick together for life and join up with other males to form bachelor groups. Each bachelor group will have its own territory and works as a team to defend it.

- A male lion may stay in charge of a pride for only about two to four years before a new dominant male or bachelor group takes over and he is forced out.

- To mark the boundary of their territory, lions will leave scratch marks, rub scent, and spray urine on bushes and trees.

- The adult members of a pride, including the dominant male, let cubs pull at their fur and chase their tails. This behavior allows the cubs to practice skills that they will need when they are hunting as adults.

- Lions cannot see color as well as people can, but they can see in the dark six times better than human beings!

- A male lion's roar can be heard 5 miles away!

- Lions sleep and rest for up to 20 hours each day. They do most of their hunting when it is dark and cool. Their hunting is not always successful, so this lifestyle allows them to save energy.

- Lions can run 30 mph over short distances.

REPRODUCTION AND YOUNG

- Females are pregnant for about 14 to 15 weeks. Unless their cubs die, they will not have another litter for about two and a half years.

- If her cubs are killed, a female will want to mate again within about four days.

- On average, two to four cubs are born in each litter.

- Newborn cubs weigh 2–4 pounds, which is as much as a chicken.

- Females give birth among thick grasses or bushes, or in rocky areas. The birth place is called a *den site*. The mother introduces the cubs to the rest of the pride when they are four to six weeks old.

- Cubs drink their mother's milk until they are six to eight months old. They begin to eat meat when they are about six weeks old.

- Cubs are dependent on their mother until they are about 16 months old.

- Females in a pride often give birth to their cubs around the same time. The babies grow up together.

- Like other cats, lionesses carry their cubs in their mouths.

GLOSSARY

ADAPTED When the bodies and lifestyles of a species of animal have changed over a very long period of time so that they are suitable for the environment in which the animals live.

AMBUSH To wait and then attack from a hidden position.

DOMINANT MALE The head male in a family or group of animals. Normally, he is the largest and strongest male, and has won his position by fighting off rivals. In lion prides, the dominant male usually fathers all the cubs.

GRASSLANDS Dry areas where the only plants that will grow are tough grasses.

MIGRATING When animals move from one area to another during different seasons of the year. Animals migrate to find new food supplies, to breed, or to move to warmer places

during the winter.

SAVANNA Grasslands where some trees and bushes grow. At certain times of the year, they are very dry. At other times, there is a lot of rain. Savanna grasslands are normally warm all year.

SCAVENGE To eat other animals' leftovers or carrion (animals that are already dead).

STALK To follow without being seen.

SUBMISSIVE When an animal is willing to give in to another animal, that is stronger or more dominant.

WILDLIFE RESERVES (protected areas) In some countries, vast areas are now protected by law as special wildlife reserves or protected areas (parks). Wild animals

live in these areas and are protected from hunters by wardens. The wardens monitor the area, making sure that there is enough grassland to feed large herds of prey animals, such as zebras and antelope. The herds provide food for predator animals such as lions. Some farming is allowed on wildlife reserves. The farmers must make sure that they leave enough land for the wild animals. They must also keep their own cattle protected. Tourists pay to visit the parks to watch and photograph the animals. This helps to bring in extra money for the local villages.

CONSERVATION

- Lions once lived wild in Africa, Asia, and southern Europe.

- The critically endangered Asiatic lion lives only in the Gir Forest National Park in India. There are fewer than 300 left!

- There are between 17,000 and 23,000 lions living wild in Africa.

- In many places in Africa, lions are losing their natural habitat as farmland and towns expand. The large herds of prey animals that the lions rely on for food disappear, and the lions turn to farm animals as a source of food. Many lions are shot by farmers.

- Big cats, such as lions and leopards, are sometimes kept in tiny cages as pets, in poorly run zoos, and as attractions in circuses or night clubs. Conservation organizations are sometimes able to rescue these big cats and move them to special reserves or sanctuaries where they can live their lives as they would in the wild.

INDEX

PICTURE CREDITS

t=top, b=bottom, c=center, l=left, r=right, OFC=outside front cover, OBC=outside back cover

Alamy: OFC, 1c, 4, 7b, 12l, 14-15, 16-17, 18, 19bl, 20-21, 22-23, 26-27t, 26-27b, OBC. Corbis: 5cl, 6l, 6lc, 8-9, 10, 11b, 13, 17tr, 19t, 24-25, 28, 29, 30, 31. Nature Picture Library: 11t.

Every effort has been made to trace the copyright holders, and we apologize in advance for any unintentional omissions. We would be pleased to insert the appropriate acknowledgements in any subsequent edition of this publication.